Amazing Canadian Kids!

What They're Doing to Make a Difference And How You Can Too!

Written by Sheneeza Kanji

authorHOUSE®

AuthorHouse™
1663 Liberty Drive
Bloomington, IN 47403
www.authorhouse.com
Phone: 1-800-839-8640

Published by AuthorHouse 01/13/2012

ISBN: 978-1-4634-2060-4 (sc)
ISBN: 978-1-4634-2061-1 (e)

Library of Congress Control Number: 2011910252

Any people depicted in stock imagery provided by Thinkstock are models, and such images are being used for illustrative purposes only. Certain stock imagery © Thinkstock.

This book is printed on acid-free paper.

Table of Contents

Introduction

"Could a greater miracle take place than for us to look through each other's eyes for an instant?" A powerful question posed by one of the great peacemakers and anti-slavery activists of his time - Henry David Thoreau would have been proud to witness this miracle he speaks of lived through the extraordinary lives of - not adults - but children.

The stories you are about to read are truly amazing. They tell of five Canadian children enjoying a normal childhood, until there came a day when their world is forever changed. What happens to transform their childhood into something unexpected and remarkable? You will witness that it is a deep sense of compassion for their environment or for people in their family, community or around the world that drives these amazing children to reach beyond all expectations to make important contributions in the lives of all those who need help. These five children possess a wonderful view of the world around us as one in which children can make a difference, regardless of age, once you set goals and work hard to achieve them. And so, each embark on the amazing journey you will soon come to know – a journey through the eyes of another.

The sense that anything is possible if we all work together to make positive changes is somehow lost to many adults. However, as we see in these stories, there are children who do not look for the *impossible* but instead seek the *possible*. You will be inspired by the sheer determination and perseverance of the amazing children you will meet in these chapters. Their stories will highlight the important and lasting contributions they have made and continue to make in the various causes they fight for. The choices each make to take steps toward improving environmental awareness or the lives of others, in turn moves others to the point where they are also inspired to take action on important issues in our world. You will meet Ryan Hreljac who believes in this "Ripple Effect" because he has seen it first hand. He believes that when you reach out to help in an important cause, no matter what it may be, you are also reaching out to inspire others to help as well.

Many of us see and hear about the suffering of people on television, in the newspapers or on the internet. But what if anything do we do about it? Do we just take a little of it in and then continue on with our lives as if it has nothing to do with us? Not so with Craig Keilburger. Craig decided that the pain of reading a disturbing newspaper article was too much for him to ignore what he had learned and could not see why he should not help victims even if they lived far away. Craig's story is testament that one person, even a child, can change the world simply by choosing not to ignore those who need our help.

Perhaps there is someone in your family or community that appears to be having a tough time. When you choose to use a talent or an interest you have in something to help that person, you may just change that persons life for the better – forever! Kayla Cornale understands this very much. Her love of the piano transformed her cousin's life, helping her cousin to overcome difficult challenges.

The idea that you can find inspiration to make a difference almost anywhere is not lost to Miranda Andersen. With the help of her teacher, she discovered she had a passion for filmmaking and used that passion to raise awareness about two of Earth's majestic ecosystems. Realizing she could combine these two interests set her off on a new and exciting path in her young life.

In our own communities and cities in Canada and around the world, we often drive or walk by individuals who seem to live on the streets. Do you ever stop to wonder what that would be like? Can you imagine yourself without a home to live in or food to eat? It would be a very sad and lonely life I'm sure. I would hope that there would be someone out there who cared enough to ask me if I needed help - someone like young Hannah Taylor who had a difficult time understanding why no one cared for these people. If more people could be driven to action as Hannah was to change the lives of these helpless individuals, perhaps there would be less of this problem.

In reading this book, I hope you come away with a sense of understanding of the many difficulties and challenges that a large number of people and environmental habitats confront everyday in our world. Most of us here in Canada live very good lives in comparison to others in this country and around our planet. The problems that these people and our world habitats face will not go away on their own. They need compassionate, caring, empathetic and determined individuals such as the five children you are about to meet, to stand up and let the world know this is unacceptable. I hope you will come to a better realization that we must work together to make it easier for those who are suffering. Let's face it, one day we may need help in some way and we would hope that someone would be there to answer our call.

To help you in your next step once you have read this book, I have provided you with two valuable sections at the end of each chapter. *What You Should Know* and *How You Can Help* offer information and suggestions to guide you along your own amazing journey of awareness and action. Simply pick one or more of the causes that you feel drawn to and begin with small goals for yourself. Friends, family, and teachers are valuable resources for helping you to achieve these goals. It is always better to start small and perhaps your ideas for change may gradually emerge into something more than what you expected. The five Canadian kids you are about to meet can certainly tell you all about that!

Enjoy!
Sheneeza Kanji
Author, *Amazing Canadian Kids! What They're Doing to Make a Difference (And How You Can Too!)*

Ryan and the Water Well

Chapter 1

"I just love hearing more examples of people who ... just do what they want to do and don't care if it's not going to fix the entire problem or not going to make the biggest impact on the world, but are naïve enough to do what I did when I was six. And it's amazing what can happen over time." Ryan Hreljac

If you ever thought that being a kid meant that you had to wait to grow up to help other kids - think again! Ryan Hreljac was a young boy who did not allow his age to stand in the way of doing the right thing. Instead, he decided he needed to make a difference immediately. At first, he appeared to be a typical child, living in a small community just outside Ottawa, Ontario. Like many Canadian kids, he enjoyed playing hockey and hanging out with his friends. But Ryan was not typical.

At just six years of age, one day at school turned out to be an amazing turning point in his young life. As he sat in his classroom, Ryan listened to his grade one teacher, Mrs. Prest, tell a story that would cause a sense of shock and disbelief to wash over him. The story she told was of people who lived in a distant land. Her words would move Ryan to the point where it would send him and his family on an important and life-saving journey to change the world – a journey that would take them from Canada to Africa, where water can take or save a life.

Mrs. Prest told Ryan's class that there were many people living in Africa who did not have access to medicine, food and clean water, as we did here in Canada. Ryan listened with sadness as his teacher spoke of how many people, especially children, become very sick and even die because they do not have clean water to drink. Mrs. Prest told her students that many people in poor and **developing countries** have to walk long distances to find water to drink, cook with and bathe in. The water they find is often brown, smelly and carries a lot of germs and harmful bacteria. After hearing that raising enough money could help to build a water well in an African village, Ryan became determined to do just that. Mrs. Prest had said that it only costs $70 to build a well that could provide a village and the surrounding area with clean and safe water. Ryan did not have $70 but he knew who did!

After school, Ryan raced home and asked his parents for the $70 to build a well in Africa but was disappointed when his mom told him she could not simply hand over that much money to him. Ryan's mom noticed his look of disappointment and suggested he raise the money himself by doing extra chores around the house. Ryan quickly agreed and set out to earn the funds he would need to build his well. His mom helped him track his earnings by posting a chart on the kitchen fridge and providing Ryan with a cookie tin to place his money in. Ryan's chores included vacuuming, washing windows, cleaning the yard and helping with the garbage. His parents even gave him five dollars for excellent grades on his report card!

Four months later, Ryan had raised the $70 he thought he needed. He and his mom decided that they would deliver the money to an organization that provides safe water in developing countries. When Ryan heard from the people at the organization that the drill to build the well would cost about $2000 more, he did not become discouraged. Instead, he decided he would do whatever it took to raise the funds needed, even if it meant doing more chores around the house. He was quite a determined child and he was not willing to give up his drive to build the well in Africa.

As he continued to do his part to raise the money for the drill, Ryan's story began to be passed on to many people. Word was spreading of an amazing little boy who was trying to do something wonderful for disadvantaged people in a far away land. Inspired by Ryan's youthful innocence and determination, many donated funds to help him build the well. Ryan was overjoyed each time he and his family were greeted with envelopes bearing donations of money and cheques in their home mailbox. He was touched by the generosity of strangers.

Eventually, Ryan's story was featured in newspapers across Canada and TV stations wanted to interview this special young boy. He soon became known in other parts of the world also. Oprah Winfrey, a famous talk-show host in the United Sates, interviewed him on her show -- twice! His message to her audience and the world was that age does not matter when there are people who need help. Anyone can help to make a difference at any age if they truly care about something.

Many more people who heard of Ryan's story from reading the newspaper or seeing him on TV were also moved by his compassion. They too began to send money to help him achieve his goal of building the well. Some people even donated their air miles so that Ryan and his parents could fly to Africa to see the well once it was completed. Due to Ryan's efforts and the kindness of strangers, all the money was raised for the drill and the well, and so construction began immediately at Angolo Primary School near the town of Agweo, in Uganda, a country in East Africa. Ryan had asked that the well be built near a school so that children could benefit from it while they were busy learning. People in the nearby towns and villages could have access to the well also.

Meanwhile, back home in Canada, Ryan's story had gained so much in popularity that he had become a famous young boy. People invited him to come and speak to their groups about his determination to build the well in Africa. His first speech in front of citizens of a local town made him quite nervous; however, he persevered and impressed the people with his story and bravery. From there, he went on to give speeches in front of larger numbers of people. He was becoming more confident and passionate as he raised awareness about his cause. He spoke at the Millennium Dreamers Conference at Walt Disney World in Florida, where he was presented with a star on the Disney Walk of Fame. In his speeches, he made sure that everyone understood how important it was that all children, no matter where they lived, have clean water to drink, instead of unsafe water carrying dangerous diseases.

Ryan's classmates wanted to get involved to help their friend as well. One way they could do so was to learn more about life for children in these developing countries. Ryan was now in grade two and he was about to gain a lasting friendship.

His teacher, Mrs. Dillabaugh, arranged for her students and the children of Angolo Primary School to connect with each other as pen pals. Ryan's pen pal was Akana Jimmy, an eight year old boy who liked to play soccer. Through his letters, Ryan learned that Jimmy lived in a house made of mud, and that he and other children had to walk 5 kilometers each way to find water for their village. Sometimes, Jimmy made that barefoot walk four or five times a day! The water was quite polluted and unsafe but they drank it because they were desperately thirsty. Jimmy learned from Ryan that Canada had plenty of clean water, something he could not fully believe. He enjoyed reading Ryan's descriptions of life in Canada - a far away place he did not think he would ever see.

Finally, there came wonderful news that Ryan's first well had been completed! More than one year later, Ryan and his parents arrived at Angolo Primary School in Uganda to see the

Ryan walks the path to his first well in Uganda

well. As they arrived near the town, they were stunned by what they were seeing and hearing. Thousands of children greeted them along the side of the road and in the village while beating drums, clapping their hands and chanting, "Ryan! Ryan! Ryan!" There was such melody and happiness in their voices. Feelings of joy and pride filled Ryan as he waved to those gathered on his behalf.

A Canadian Television crew followed Ryan and his family as they walked down the path towards the school. As he arrived closer to the well, Ryan was approached by a tall smiling boy whose name was Akana Jimmy – his special pen pal! The boys were both very excited to finally meet each other in person. It was obvious that their letters had already created a lasting bond between them. They turned and walked to the well together and read the message engraved on the stone at the base of the well: "Funded by Ryan H., for the Community of Angolo Primary School".

Since the well has been built the children of Angolo Primary School are stronger and healthier. They now have clean water for cooking and bathing with, and for drinking. There is far less danger of becoming very ill or dying from being exposed to the dangers of unsafe water. These grateful children will never forget what Ryan did for them. "Water is life for us", said the Principal of the school. Ryan understands this very much. His dream that day was for everyone in Africa to have access to clean water, something that is so important to the health and survival of many people.

Ryan and Jimmy meet at the well

When Ryan returned home to Canada, he thought of his special friend and pen-pal, Jimmy, quite often. Until one day, Ryan and his family heard worrisome news that the situation in northern Uganda was becoming quite dangerous. There was a lot of **conflict** in the country placing children at great risk of becoming hurt or even killed. One night, there was a raid by a rebel group in Jimmy's village and he was taken to be trained as a child soldier. However, Jimmy escaped and found refuge with a friend. This friend contacted Ryan's family in Canada. Ryan was quite nervous for his pen-pal and so his parents decided to do something extraordinary to help. They made arrangements for Jimmy to come to Canada and he eventually became a permanent member of their family!

After much planning, Ryan's friend arrived in the country that he had heard so much about. There was great joy as the family and Jimmy celebrated the reunion. Everyone, including friends, helped to make Jimmy's new life comfortable and happy. He may have missed his homeland of Africa, but he was grateful for the amazing opportunity to live in Canada. Jimmy and Ryan were pen pals whose bond was sealed at a well in Uganda, and who had now become brothers!

Ryan and Jimmy in Uganda during Ryan's first visit

Today, Ryan continues to follow his dream of clean water for everyone in developing countries around the world. He is a tall teenager attending to his university studies. He works very hard to balance his school work and work for his organization, The Ryan's Well Foundation. He continues to raise awareness of the need for clean water and sanitation in the poorest regions of the world. He has spoken to millions of people and met important individuals, all of whom have been moved and inspired by his message. Children in countries around the world have told Ryan how they are also trying to follow in his footsteps by raising money and awareness for clean water for all those who need it the most. In fact, some of his largest donations so far have been contributed by children!

Ryan is proud to say that the Ryan's Well Foundation has raised millions of dollars and built over 600 wells in sixteen countries throughout

Teenage Ryan visits one of the wells built by The Ryan's Well Foundation in Uganda

Africa and other parts of the developing world, including Haiti. There are hundreds of thousands of people who are very grateful to Ryan for all his hard work and for caring about them. If not for his determination in overcoming challenges and the compassion that he has shown to people who desperately need clean water, many more would suffer illness and death. Imagine a six year old child may have saved many lives by simply taking action on an important and worthwhile cause!

Ryan's story has testified that all it takes is one person - even a young child - who cares enough to make a difference. If you imagine that he dropped a stone onto a clear, clean surface of water and observed how the ripples from that one small stone spread out, like people joining together toward a great and important cause, you will see the far reaching results – many more water wells being built for those who need it. The Ryan's Well Foundation guides this "ripple effect" spirit in helping to inspire other children, as well as their parents and teachers to take action and make a difference in their own way. By doing so, each will observe their own "ripple effect".

What You Should Know:

More than one in six people worldwide – 894 million – do not have access to safe freshwater.

Around 1.1 billion people globally do not have access to improved water supply sources, whereas 2.4 billion people do not have access to any type of improved sanitation facility.

Unsafe water, inadequate sanitation and insufficient hygiene are the major

Photo by Filomena Scalise (FreeDigitalPhotos.net)

risk factors for disease, which is the second leading contributor to the global burden of disease. For children under 15, this burden is greater than the combined impact of HIV/AIDS, malaria and tuberculosis.

About 2 million people die every year due to diarrheal disease; most of them are children less than 5 years of age. The most affected are the populations in developing countries, living in extreme conditions of poverty.

At least $7 billion per year is needed to improve water and sanitation in impoverished countries.

Improvements in sanitation and drinking water could reduce the number of children who die from water-related illness each year by 2.2 million.

Access to clean water and sanitation helps to sustain communities, build livelihoods, and save lives.

How You Can Help:

Brainstorm ideas with your family, friends and classmates for raising funds to help build a well through Ryan's Well Foundation (www.ryanswell.ca). You may consider inviting friends to your party and instead of gifts have them bring donations to drop into a "well". Your party could have a water theme where you play water games and discuss the importance of water in our lives.

You may also consider having your school/classmates raise funds as Ryan first did. "Dollars for Chores" could be collected in a jar at home with a chart posted on the fridge tracking the amount earned. Once you reach a certain amount determined by you and your peers (perhaps $20) bring your jars to school. The class that brings in their jars first could win a pizza party or an afternoon of their choosing.

Organize a "Walk for a Well" or a "Run for a Well" in honour of the hundreds of thousands of women and children who walk many kilometers each day to find water for their families. Your event will raise awareness and funds to help build a well.

Hold a street/community garage sale in your neighbourhood and donate proceeds to build a well.

You can also raise awareness of the need for clean water and sanitation in many parts of the world through speeches and projects at school. Discuss how we can help at home by conserving water.

You can ask your principal to allow your school to partner with Ryan's Well Foundation and join the Youth in Action Program. Your school can be a part of a School Challenge Project as well (see website for details).

Ryan's story is a wonderful example of how teachers can inspire their students to do great things when they chose to raise and discuss important social issues. Read a story, ask a question and begin the discussion. You too can inspire someone to do something wonderful!

www.ryanswell.ca

To find out more about children affected by armed conflict visit www.unicef.org/voy/ (search "child soldiers").

Ryan chatting with a young child in Johannesburg, South Africa

Miranda Films for the Environment

"My films have won a lot of awards but the best award for me for making a movie is to have someone change the way they do things that effect their environment or make them think about how they can do one thing to help change the world." **Miranda Andersen**

Oceans and forests stretch out across vast portions of the Earth bringing with them key elements to nurture and sustain life on this planet. These majestic **biomes** are therefore in need of our constant attention for the significant role they play in the cycle of life. We are at a point where we cannot afford to ignore the harm that is being brought to them as a result of our human activities.

All life depends heavily on the oceans and forests of the world for one very important thing – oxygen! We simply cannot live without it. In addition to supplying the air we breathe, these large habitats and ecosystems provide many valuable ingredients that nourish and support human and animal life. From them we harness food, medicine and we build our livelihoods around all that they have to offer. We use oceans for fishing, for transportation and for recreation. We need forests mainly for their trees which help to build our homes and provide us with paper products.

These ecosystems are home to much of the plant and animal life on the planet that we as humans depend on greatly. But these are only a few of the significant ways that oceans and forests sustain all life. There is one more very important way that they help us.

Both of these natural ecosystems absorb much of the carbon dioxide in our atmosphere and therefore help to offset the harmful effects of global warming. In fact, much of the waste that human beings produce contributes to these excessive amounts of harmful gases that exist in the air we breathe. So you see, without oceans and forests, living things on our planet would not be able to survive. The question is then, *If all life depends so heavily on these ecosystems, why are we as human beings not taking better care to protect them just as they help and protect us?* This question is asked and acted upon by many people in our world. However, much work is needed if we are going to succeed in taking better care of what gives us life. More people, especially children and youth, are getting involved in raising awareness of the plight of the world's valuable biomes and their ecosystems. One such young lady is doing her part to change the world and educate others about how we treat our oceans and forests, as well as the living things that call them home.

Miranda Andersen loves the ocean and the wilderness. Perhaps this love was born out of the fact that she has lived near them all her life. With her family, and during school with her classmates, she has spent countless hours exploring the natural environment around her community of Port Moody, which sits just on the

Miranda and Ruth Foster at the Mossom Creek Hatchery

outskirts of Vancouver, British Columbia. This love of nature and especially the ocean near her home, led young Miranda to the Mossom Creek Hatchery where she would spend her Sunday mornings volunteering with Ruth Foster, one of the founders of the community salmon hatchery. Miranda and Ruth developed a bond out of their mutual love of "protecting all things environmental". Miranda began to see Ruth as a true hero – her hero!

It seemed obvious then that when Miranda's grade four teacher, Jen Whiffin, asked her class to write about someone they admired—a hero – Miranda would choose Ruth. "I really urged them to select heroes that went beyond famous heroes, particularly ones that were doing amazing local work," says Ms. Whiffin. She hoped that by connecting directly with their hero, that the writing task would spark a sense of **social responsibility** and inspiration in her students. The assignment took on an interesting twist when she suggested that some of her students use Apple's Mac computer **iMovie** program to tell their hero stories. The students had not had any experience with this type of filmmaking technology, but with the help of their teacher and lots of perseverance, the students, and particularly Miranda, produced works they were quite proud of. Without realizing it, Miranda's teacher was developing an environmental filmmaker in her young student.

Miranda's film featured an interview with Ruth where we learn about a term coined by environmental educators called *Nature Deficit Disorder*. In the interview, Ruth expresses concern that many children are not truly in touch with nature or the natural environment around where they live, partly due to the fact that they rely heavily on indoor activities such as electronic games and television to entertain them in their spare time. Ruth feels that we tend to care about things that we learn about. By feeding and caring for the salmon in the hatchery, Miranda learned about rearing and releasing salmon in an effort to preserve salmon habitats.

In addition, she learned that she could make a difference, just as all the other volunteers at the hatchery were. Ruth and other environmental educators are worried that many kids are "losing touch with the environment" and are hoping that by exploring, investigating and learning more about the natural world, the current generation of young people will begin to care about what they learn and perhaps act more on it. By giving Ruth a voice to express these concerns, Miranda was doing her part to educate others.

Ms. Whiffin was quite happy with Miranda's film project on her hero and decided that it should be entered into a film contest for young people. The *MyHero Film Festival*, based out of California in the United States, invites people of all ages to submit short films on certain topics. Miranda's film on Ruth was a great candidate for the elementary school category, and so her teacher submitted it with Miranda's parents' permission. Not long after, word came that not only had Miranda's film been selected as a finalist, but it had actually won the competition! Miranda and her family were invited to make a trip to California to receive her award and meet other filmmakers who were also making a difference with their own films. Miranda was even more pleased when she received a letter of recognition from the *David Suzuki Foundation* for her film. Ms. Whiffin believes that, "The most critical component of being a good filmmaker, is having a sense of the story that you want to tell and how you tell it well using video." With patience, Miranda was learning to master this important skill.

These amazing acknowledgements for her efforts were great vehicles for driving Miranda's ambitions further. She was able to see first-hand how her film demonstrated the power of one person to make a difference. Miranda could use her films to raise more awareness and educate more people about the importance of caring for and preserving environmental habitats. She began to submit other films, such as *Making a Difference*, a one and half minute silent film on how one person—Ruth—was making a difference while asking others if they are doing anything to make a difference. This film won *Best in Fest* by a film contest sponsored by *Earth Day Canada*. The win awarded Miranda a trip to Toronto, Ontario and a vacation to anywhere in North America!

In addition to developing a passion for environmental filmmaking, Miranda was capturing the attention of peers, teachers and judges with her public speaking as part of school competitions. Ruth had introduced her to the concept of **electronic waste** which immediately sparked Miranda's interest and sent her on another quest to research and write on this new topic. Miranda was quite upset to learn that electronic waste (or **e-waste**) is often shipped overseas to countries like Africa, India and China and that impoverished peoples and even children in these countries, dismantle the **toxic** parts, placing themselves and their health in harm's way. Finding this quite sad and unacceptable, Miranda decided she needed to raise awareness through a school public speech competition and went further by holding an e-waste collection during *Earth Day* celebrations in her community where she set up a booth for people to drop off their unwanted electronics, such as old computers and cell phones, for the organization *Free Geek*. Her efforts were quite successful as she collected enough

e-waste to fill several cars and an SUV! In addition, she was awarded a finalist in her school's speech competition for her work on this troubling topic.

It was during this time that Miranda began to connect with Dr. Mary Hagedorn, a

Miranda showcases Free Geek and the hazards of e-waste at a local salmon release festival

marine biologist. Dr. Mary is a scientist with the Smithsonian Institution in Washington D.C. in the United States who works from the University of Hawaii. In Hawaii, on the island of Oahu, she is doing important work with the ocean's coral. As Miranda learned more about Mary's work, she realized that another film would be necessary and that meant a trip to Hawaii to meet this amazing scientist.

Prior to her trip to the island and meeting Mary, Miranda researched everything she possibly could on the ocean's coral and the work that was being done in Hawaii to save and protect them. She developed "just the right" interview questions for Dr. Mary and then set out to produce her next environmental film. On the island, Miranda and Mary spent a day together, talking about coral and its importance in the life of oceans and the planet. Miranda learned that the oceans pull down carbon dioxide from the air and when there is an excessive amount of this gas in the atmosphere it puts a burden on the coral. How does it do this? Dr. Mary wants us to think of the ocean as a sink for carbon dioxide. As the oceans absorb the carbon dioxide it causes them to become more acidic, which in turn is creating a problem for the coral. It is just as adding carbon dioxide to water transforms the water into soda, causing it to become more acidic than water. This acid is harmful to our teeth because it erodes the enamel. Likewise, carbon dioxide being absorbed by oceans is causing the oceans to become acidic and may erode coral structures, causing them to die and disappear. Miranda found this very disturbing, especially as she realized that billions of sea creatures depend on coral for their homes and nurseries as well. She also

Miranda with Dr. Mary Hagedorn in Hawaii

learned that many other human activities may be destroying this important world biome.

Miranda's film *Help Mary Save the Coral*, named after Dr. Mary's website, brought to light many of these concerns, as well as explained what Mary and the Hawaii Institute of Marine Biology at the University of Hawaii are doing to save the coral of the world. The work involves an amazing concept called **cryobiology** that involves studying the effects of low temperatures on living things. In doing this, scientists such as Mary are able to create a "frozen bank of coral sperm and embryonic cells from coral species", storing them until they are ready to be thawed. What they are really doing is preserving coral in order to replenish and relocate these valuable ecosystems to new areas in the ocean to "jump start" new coral reefs. This way, they may be able to offset some of the local and global threats facing coral and possibly reseed the oceans for the future! Not surprisingly, Miranda's efforts to raise awareness on this important topic through a series of documentary films earned her additional awards and recognitions, including the *Unsung Hero Award* from *Children Uniting Nations* in California. At this point, Miranda was only 11 years old!

Miranda was building quite a reputation as a talented young environmental filmmaker. She spent two years on a youth film jury in Vancouver, judging other films by her filmmaking peers. She had begun to jot down ideas for other films in her journal. One such idea came at the inspiration of a speech she wrote as a school project. Miranda had learned that some of the main pollutants that were causing harm to oceanic life were the enormous amount of plastic and other garbage discarded by humans. Another inspiration occurred when she came upon a woman in Vancouver who was attempting to live "plastic free" by substituting plastic habits with more eco-friendly ones such as using metal straws instead of those made of plastic and carrying along stainless steel containers for restaurant leftovers. Miranda herself adapted these ideas into her own life and convinced those around her to do the same. She titled her speech *The Great Pacific Garbage Patch* which highlighted these concerns and then went on to create her next film, *Plastic Forever*. She earned a silver medal for her speech and first place in another *MyHero* filmmaking contest for her film! She was gaining more confidence in her ability to be a vehicle for environmental change with each new accomplishment.

Miranda's focus on the plight of the world's oceans gave way to a new focus on the forests of our world when one day, as she was walking to the library in her community, she was horrified to see a man painting a tree blue. Yes, blue! Upon further investigation, she learned that the man was an Australian artist and environmentalist working in Vancouver to inspire **social action** through art. He was actually attempting to raise awareness about **global deforestation**. He painted the trees blue—using paint safe for the trees and the animals that call them home – to, among other things, symbolize the colour that we turn when we are unable to breathe. He was sending this powerful message not just in Vancouver, but in other cities around the world as well! His passion and work captured Miranda's interest and led to yet another film—this one appropriately titled, *Blue Trees*. During this project, Miranda realized that she had a connection with this artist. Her own films were a form of art – social art. She did not paint trees blue. Rather, she created films—a form of art—to raise awareness about important social or environmental issues in the hopes of inspiring others into social action as well.

Blue Trees allowed Miranda the opportunity to learn more about the frustration of deforestation around the world. It is well known that the trees of our world are really the lungs of the earth, soaking up carbon dioxide through the process of **photosynthesis** and returning healthy oxygen to the atmosphere.

Just as corals and oceans, trees and forests have existed on earth since before the coming of human beings. Sadly, it was when humans arrived on the planet that these amazing ecosystems began to suffer. Today, with the increase of human population (we're close to 7 billion!), the stress that our habits are placing on oceans and forests are threatening our health, global climate and the existence of future generations. Miranda's film reminds us that although we gain in some way when trees are cut, the cutting down of trees for livelihood must be managed in an environmentally friendly manner to ensure their protection, especially for our future and the future of the animals who call forests their home.

Today, Miranda is twelve years old and has received much recognition for her work. Her achievements have been profiled in newspaper and magazine articles and she has been invited to speak to groups of people about her passion. She continues to gain inspiration for new film ideas through the amazing people she meets who are doing wonderful work to protect "all things environmental".

A tropical forest scenery (courtesy of mack2happy, freedigitalphotos.com)

Ruth Foster, Mary Hagedorn, her teacher Jen Whiffin, the support of her parents and many other individuals have contributed to sparking a sense of social awareness and responsibility in this young environmentalist. Meeting challenges with patience and perseverance, Miranda was able to see her passion in filmmaking and public speaking, and use these talents for a greater and worthwhile good. Her message to all kids, no matter what age, is, "Get your friends, family and relatives involved in your cause. Tell your teacher or write to your politician. Find others who think like you do and come up with a club or a way to work together. If there's something you are an expert about, maybe there's something you can do with that information. And you don't have to accomplish everything you want to do at once." Miranda has chosen to use her talents and her voice as a vehicle to drive change. Never underestimate the power that you have to do the same!

What You Should Know:

According to the United Nations Environment Programme (UNEP), "Human well-being depends on the health of ecosystems. An ecosystem is a dynamic complex of plants, animals, **microorganisms** and their nonliving environment, of which people are an integral part. The benefits that we derive from nature and rely on every day, from timber and food to water and climate regulation, are all ecosystem services."

Coral reefs are in crisis and are dying at an alarming rate worldwide. Threats to the world's coral reefs include pollution, disease, overfishing and rising ocean temperatures.

Called the "rainforests of the sea," coral reefs are the greatest expression of ocean life, and one of the most **biodiverse** ecosystems on Earth. "Coastal waters account for just 7% of the total area of the ocean. However, the productivity of ecosystems such as coral reefs mean that this small area forms the basis of the world's primary fishing grounds, supplying an estimated 50% of the world's fisheries. Coastal regions provide important nutrition for close to 3 billion people, as well as 50% of animal protein and minerals to 400 million people of the least developed countries in the world." That means that if we allow coral reefs to be destroyed, we are also allowing the plants, minerals and fish that rely on coral, and that many people depend on for their existence, to be destroyed as well.

Ocean scenery off the coast of Thailand (courtesy of Sura Nualpradid, freedigitalphotos.com)

Blue, Green, Black and Brown Carbon? Blue carbon refers to carbon captured by the world's oceans. Green carbon is carbon removed by photosynthesis and stored in the plants and soil of natural ecosystems. Of all the green carbon captured annually in the world, over half (55%) is captured by marine living organisms. Brown and black carbon emissions are from **fossil fuels**, **biofuels** and wood burning and are major contributors to global warming.

Deforestation now accounts for over 20% of global **greenhouse gas** emissions.

The biggest driver of global deforestation is agriculture. Farmers cut forests to provide more room for planting crops or grazing livestock. Often many small farmers will each clear a few acres to feed their families by cutting down trees and burning them in a process known as "slash and burn" agriculture.

70% of Earth's land animals and plants live in forests, and many cannot survive the deforestation that destroys their homes. Some of these plant and animal species are therefore in danger of **extinction**.

The world is consuming more and more electronic products every year. This has caused a dangerous explosion in electronic scrap (e-waste) containing toxic chemicals and heavy metals that cannot be disposed of or recycled safely. But this problem can be avoided. Environmental organizations such as *GreenPeace* are pressing leading electronic companies to produce more "greener electronics".

The rearing and releasing of salmon in places like Mossom Creek in Port Moody, British Columbia is important because it reintroduces salmon that had left, back into the area, thereby strengthening the surrounding ecosystems. When an animal species leaves or dies out from an ecosystem, it tends to change the entire ecosystem.

How You Can Help:

There are many environmental issues that you can find out more about by researching through books, the internet and by asking questions. Here are a few that you may want to investigate:

Marine Biodiversity	Carbon Cycle	Preserving and Protecting Ecosystems
Global Deforestation	Global Warming and Climate Change	
Natural Disasters	Human Population	Wildlife Conservation
Importance of Coral Reefs	Greenhouse Gas Emissions	Electronic Waste

As Miranda's story has demonstrated, you can use an interest or a talent that you have to take action on a social or environmental issue that you feel strongly about. You may even discover a talent or an interest you did not know existed within you! Use this energy towards a great cause and you can do your part to make a difference.

You may raise awareness about your favourite environmental issues through speeches and projects at school, just as Miranda has done.

Visit conservation areas in your community. Whether you live near small ecosystems such as ponds or large ones such as oceans and forests, you can explore with care, and learn more about your natural world.

Volunteer your time in helping to preserve and protect ecosystems and habitats in your area.

Use eco-friendly and/or green products as much as possible in your everyday life.

Do your part to reduce, reuse and recycle! Miranda has learned of another "r" – "refuse"! Advocate for your school and home to be eco-friendly, and refuse products and habits that are not.

(courtesy of digitalart, freedigitalphotos.com)

Miranda suggests:

Books: *Story of Stuff Series* – author, Annie Leonard (Simon and Schuster Canada)

Saving Planet Earth – author, Tony Juniper (HarperCollins Canada)

Get Real: What Kind of World Are You Buying – author, Mara Rockliff (Running Press)

Oceans—The Threats to Our Seas and What You Can Do to Turn the Tide – author, Jon Bowermaster (Public Affairs with Participant Media)

DVDs: *Planet Earth Series* (BBC, directed by Alastair Fothergill)

Eco Pirate – The Story of Paul Watson (Entertainment One; Written, Produced, Directed by Trish Dolman)

For more information on:

The Mossom Creek Hatchery in Port Moody, British Columbia visit *mossomcreek.org*.

Dr. Mary Hagedorn's work on the world's coral visit her renamed website *coralrecovery.org*.

Electronic Waste and how you can help visit *freegeekvancouver. org* or *freegeektoronto.org*.

Websites and links to many environmental causes for teachers, children and youth visit *www.ecokids.ca* and *www.nrdc.org/ reference/kids.asp* (U.S. site).

Further Reading:

Our Living Earth: A Story of People, Ecology, and Preservation – author, Yann Arthus Bertrand (Abrams Books for Young Readers)

Our Choice: How We Can Solve the Climate Crisis – author, Al Gore (Puffin Books)

The New 50 Simple Things Kids Can Do To Save The Earth – The Earthworks Group (Andrews McMeel Publishing, LLC)

See inside Planet Earth – authors, Katie Daynes and Peter Allen (Usborne Publishing Ltd.)

Hannah Cares for the Homeless

Chapter 3

"The thing I hope, deep in my heart, is that everyone will see homeless people as people. They are just like you and me but they have just fallen on hard times." Hannah Taylor

At just five years of age, Hannah Taylor discovered something very sad as she drove along a street in Winnipeg, Manitoba with her mom on a bitterly cold winter's day. As their car passed by a back alley, Hannah peered over and saw a man searching through a garbage container. When she witnessed the man eating something he found in the garbage, she became quite confused and asked her mother why he was doing that. Her mother's answer would send a wave of sadness flooding through Hannah's heart, and set in motion the amazing drive of a young girl to change the lives of some of the forgotten and disadvantaged peoples of our world – the homeless and hungry.

Hannah listened as her mother explained that the man was homeless and "down on his luck". It was a shocking answer for Hannah who, at her young age, had not experienced poverty before. As her mother described what a homeless person was, Hannah felt her heart tug painfully. In the days and months following this emotional first experience with homelessness,

Hannah began to worry about the man she saw, wondering where he was and if he was okay. Was he still homeless? Was he still searching for food to eat? Was he sad and scared? Who was he and where was his family? The questions she asked herself and her mother did not seem to have the answers she was looking for. But there was one question she asked particularly often during that year that finally led her mother to offer a suggestion.

Hannah's mother had explained that homeless people do not have enough money and so they live outside, having to search for food and a warm place to rest their head when they want to sleep. Their entire day is spent trying to survive, which is even harder in the winter months, when cold and wind makes it dangerous and difficult to try to stay alive. "Why?" asked Hannah. "Why, Why, Why?" Why did these people not have a home to go to and food to eat just as she did? It was a simple question but Hannah's mother did not have the answer, and so she gave a life-changing piece of advice to her young daughter. "Hannah," her mother said one night before bed, "sometimes when you worry and feel sad about things, if you do something to change the problem, your heart won't feel so sad".

Even at her young age, Hannah realized what her mother had told her was that if you see a problem you should try to be a part of the solution, and that by doing something to help, you will feel very happy. So when on her way to school, she saw another homeless person pushing a grocery cart full of her belongs down the street, Hannah made the amazing decision to help "cure" homelessness and hunger. She was not sure how she was going to do it, but she did not let her age stand in the way. She knew she had to do something to help make a difference.

Hannah's amazing journey to help raise awareness and money for people without a home or enough food to eat began with her grade one class. Confident and determined, Hannah asked her teacher if she could speak to the class about something important. She explained to her classmates what she had learned and experienced about homeless people. This speech to raise awareness was the beginning of many more she would give. It would inspire her peers to get involved as well. Together they decided that they would raise money through art and bake sales, hold clothing drives and raise awareness with their families and friends. They would donate all the money and clothes to a homeless shelter in their community. At six years of age, they were very successful in their efforts!

Hannah had always loved ladybugs. For her, these small insects were a symbol of good luck. So when she started to collect spare coins for the homeless in baby food jars she found in her kitchen, she decided that she should paint them red and black to resemble ladybugs. This would bring good luck to her efforts to raise money and to the homeless people she would donate it to. Hannah hoped her ladybug jars would "make change" for these special people and that is just what they did.

Hannah painted her first 150 ladybugs all by herself! Eventually, she and members of her family and friends would

 paint and decorate the ladybug jars together, enjoying the part where they could paint black dots over the red paint. From these crafty jars and Hannah's desire to take action on a serious problem, *The Ladybug Foundation* was born. Hannah was eight years old, and dropping off the jars to various businesses and schools around Winnipeg would be the first experience that many more people would have with the amazing passion of a young girl to "make change" for the homeless.

Hannah then decided she would like to meet some of the homeless people she was trying to help. During one of her first visits to a **homeless mission** with her parents, Hannah's eyes met those of a man sitting nearby. He seemed sad and lonely, perhaps even shy. Hannah walked over to him and they talked for a while. She learned that his name was Rick and that he came to the mission for food and shelter. When Hannah leaned over and hugged him tightly, the warmth and love that poured from her heart made him cry. They were "happy tears," he said. He could not remember the last time someone had showed him they cared in such a way. From that moment on, a very special friendship developed and Rick would be a part of Hannah's life. His face and his story would help to guide *The Ladybug Foundation* on their journey to raise money and awareness for homeless

shelters and programs across Canada.

As Hannah and Rick's story spread throughout the country, many schools and organizations began to contact the Foundation asking if Hannah would come to speak to them about her passion for the disadvantaged peoples living among us. With each speech she gave, Hannah became more passionate and confident about the cause she was championing. We see her compassion as she tells all those gathered, "The thing I hope, deep in my heart, is that everyone will see homeless people as people. They are just like you and me but they have just fallen on hard times."

During a speech in Winnipeg, Rick was there to tell everyone what his experience as a homeless person has been. People heard about the sadness, loneliness and helplessness that homeless individuals feel from someone who knew exactly what it is like, because he has lived it. They heard that what he needed was someone to show him they cared about him and that they wanted to help him. Hannah was that person for him, but there were many other homeless people - some who may be families with children - who need people to do for them what Hannah did for Rick. They need someone to give them hope and another chance.

The Ladybug Foundation became a charitable organization, raising awareness and money, and donating it to various homeless shelters across Canada. Big Boss Lunches began when Hannah decided that it would be better to gather the "Big Bosses" from all the businesses around Winnipeg in one place rather than trying to meet with each of them individually about helping her and the Foundation to achieve their goals. When she held the lunches and invited all the "bosses", she could speak to many of them at one time and ask for their donations.

For her first Big Boss Lunch Hannah used her love of drawing to raise money. She drew an amazing 50 pictures to sell at her auction! When one of the "Big Bosses" stood up and asked Hannah how much her pictures were selling for, she answered, "Whatever amount is in your heart to give." This beautiful answer would motivate many of the "Bosses" to give generously. One of her pictures of a ladybug sold for $10,000 when two "bosses" both decided they wanted it and began a bidding competition. What good luck her drawings had brought to the Foundation! Big Boss Lunches are now held all over Canada in cities like Toronto, Calgary, Edmonton and Winnipeg. So far they have proved to be a very successful and creative idea in fundraising.

At ten years of age, Hannah decided to use her love of writing stories to create a ladybug character named Ruby who felt very lucky. One day on her way to school, Ruby noticed a homeless bug asking for help and so she decided to do something to make a difference in the bug's life. By helping the homeless bug, Ruby the ladybug and all of "Buggyville" were changed forever. Hannah's story, *Ruby's Hope* inspires children to care about the people in their communities that need help, especially when they see through beautiful illustrations, how helping made everyone in "Buggyville" feel happy in their heart. *The Ladybug Foundation* published Hannah's amazing story of compassion in the bug world in the hopes of getting this message of helping the homeless and hungry across to the human world. Hannah was now an author.

As she continued her work on behalf of those without food or a home, Hannah's strong message of helping spread throughout the country as she spoke to more groups of people. One of the largest groups she spoke to totaled 16, 000 people! But she does not ever allow the numbers to scare her. Whether she speaks to a group of kids her own age or a group of wealthy business people, she speaks with confidence and passion. She is sure to tell everyone something very important to her heart. "I know some people are afraid of homeless people," she declared during a speech in Toronto. "But, they are great people wrapped in old clothes with sad hearts. Don't be afraid of them, be kind to them. If they're cold, share your mitts. If they're sad, give them a smile. If they're hungry, give them a sandwich." Her empathy for the forgotten people living on the streets of many towns and cities across Canada is quite amazing. Of course, as with all strangers, children must be very careful to be with a parent before approaching a homeless individual.

Since beginning *The Ladybug Foundation*, Hannah has won many awards and met many people, including the Prime Minister of Canada. She has even had the honour of a homeless shelter in Winnipeg named after her. *Hannah's Place* is warm and safe, allowing those that do not have a place to live to find comfort and a meal to eat. There are three sections in this emergency shelter. One section is for women and children; one is for youths and another for men. Hannah is proud to have such an important place named after her. She knows that all the people she has met and all the awards she has won are because she has cared about these special people.

Although she misses several days of school every month to travel on her speaking tours and to hold fundraisers for the Foundation, Hannah is a normal kid who enjoys spending time with her friends and siblings. One of her favourite places to visit is her grandmother's. She feels she may have developed some of her drive to help others from her "Nanna" who has always showed compassion and love for everyone.

Hannah also spends time building on her love of writing. She has created an internet **blog** to let her supporters know what is going on in her life. She is also using her love of sled dogs to write an inspirational true story of a blind sled dog from Churchill, Manitoba, whose owners saw beyond her handicap through to her value as a living being. It is quite possible that we can also look forward to her writing more about "Ruby, the ladybug".

Amazingly, Hannah has also helped to develop an education program that schools around the world can use to educate and inspire children to care about the issues surrounding homelessness. Her program is called *makeChange* because children and teachers will learn ways that they may become involved to change the world for better. Stories and videos shed light on the hardships that homeless individuals face everyday, as well as highlight the dreams they have for themselves, such as the dream to one day have a home to call their own. Hannah would like this program, as well as the example of her own story, to be a message to all kids that, "If you believe something in your heart and you try with all your might, you can help our world be better no matter how old you are."

Today, Hannah is fifteen years old and has raised more than $2 million dollars for various homeless shelters and programs across Canada. Recently, she was named one of the most *Transformational Canadians* by one of Canada's leading newspaper organizations, *The Globe and Mail*. This honour is awarded to a select group of Canadians who have placed great effort on improving the lives of others through their passion, determination and achievements. Hannah is also working as Canada's representative for the *World's Children's Prize for the Rights of the Child*. These groups of children – all under the age of 18 – meet annually in Sweden to raise awareness and discuss **humanitarian** issues effecting children around the world.

It is clear that Hannah holds a busy schedule and that through it all, she remains true to herself, believing in the human spirit and what it can achieve if people just cared for one another. It is quite amazing that she balances her responsibilities of school with that of her efforts to make a difference in the lives of her fellow human beings with such a high degree of success. As she looks to the future, Hannah is determined to continue her important and rewarding work in the hopes of "curing" homelessness and hunger throughout Canada and the world.

What You Should Know:

About Homelessness in Canada:

Canada's homeless population is somewhere between 200,000 and 300,000 people.

Poverty is the leading cause of homelessness in Canada.

Photo by Maggie Smith
(FreeDigitalPhotos.net)

Canada's "new homeless" are families, women, students, immigrants, aboriginals and are simply low-income Canadians who need **affordable housing.**

Many homeless emergency shelters in Canada fill to **capacity** during dangerously cold periods in the winter.

Possibly the best way to address homelessness is to help prevent **low-income** Canadians from having to make hard choices between buying food or paying for shelter.

Other common reasons for homelessness are **financial** difficulties and family problems.

Some homeless individuals **abuse** alcohol and drugs to deal with their emotional pain. With proper help and treatment, this can be prevented.

About Homelessness around the World:

There are over 1 billion homeless people on our planet who are either homeless or do not have access to proper housing or shelter.

The majority of the global homeless are women and children.

According to the United Nations, every human being has a right to proper shelter or housing as stated in Article 25 (1) of the *Universal Declaration of Human Rights.*

How You Can Help:

You, your classmates and family can get involved by researching the issue of homelessness in Canada and around the world. Often, people do not understand how big a problem is until they spend time learning about the issue. Brainstorm ideas to help "cure" homelessness.

At school and at home, role play so that you may imagine for a while what it would be like if you were homeless. How would you feel? What would you do to find shelter and food? Where would you go for help? What choices would you make to improve your situation? How would you like people to treat you?

Brainstorm ideas for fundraisers at your school. Ideas may include having students and teachers donate a glass jar from a "Dollar Store" large enough to fill with items such as pencils, erasers, small note pads, comic books, a deck of cards, and stickers. The jars can then be sold back to teachers and students for a small price of $2 per jar. All the proceeds may be donated to *The Ladybug Foundation* where your contribution will benefit the homeless and hungry.

Hold an "Art Sale for the Homeless" at your school or during a community event. Have children draw pictures to sell as Hannah did during her first "Big Boss Lunch". Donate proceeds to a homeless shelter in your community.

Read Hannah's book, *Ruby's Hope* (www.McNallyRobinson.com) and think about the characters involved. Create your own characters and story using homelessness and hunger as your theme. Share your story with others who have done the same thing during a "book club chat". How have each of you told the same story but in different ways? How were your stories similar? What important issues were seen in the stories? How did the characters feel about what was happening? How was homelessness and hunger "cured", if at all, in your stories?

Ask your principal if your school can be a part of *The Ladybug Foundation* Education Program called *makeChange* where you will learn more about the issues surrounding homelessness and hunger in Canada and throughout the world. You will have an opportunity to make a difference in the lives of people who are in need of your help. Check out *The Ladybug Foundation* website for details on the program and other ideas. www.ladybugfoundation.ca

Kayla Opens a Window for World of Autism

Chapter 4

"If you have an idea, go with it! No matter what it is - lean on family, friends, and teachers to help in any way." Kayla Cornale

Kayla Cornale grew up in a large supportive family with thirteen cousins to keep each other amused and entertained at family gatherings. The cousins often listened to music, watched TV, or explored tunes on the piano. However, during these times, Kayla observed that one of her younger cousins, Lorena, did not seem to play and communicate as the rest did. Lorena was different. With the help of doctors, Lorena's parents would soon come to realize that their daughter was caught up in a world known only to her – a world called **autism**.

As Kayla observed her cousin she noticed that Lorena had a lot of problems communicating and playing with the other children in their large family. Lorena was now seven years old and she did not seem to know how to read and write as other children her age should. "She repeated certain words over and over again," observed Kayla. Lorena continually experienced difficulty expressing and understanding her emotions and that of others. She also referred to herself in the third person as "she" instead of "me".

However, Lorena seemed to display a strong connection to music. She enjoyed songs on CDs, movies with musical themes, and she seemed to remember lyrics to songs as well. Due to these observations, Kayla decided she possibly could do something to help Lorena with some of the problems she faced. She would use her cousin's love of music as a window to open up a whole new world for her.

Kayla's idea to help Lorena led her to research autism to learn more about what her cousin was going through. She found that autistic children are not usually diagnosed with this **developmental** problem until the age of three or four when parents and other care-givers notice that the child is not behaving as children their age usually do. Speech, language, **social interaction** with others, and certain sounds in their environment usually cause these children some difficulties. However, Kayla's research confirmed that, like Lorena, many autistic children seem to enjoy music and that some even appear to have musical talents or gifts.

Kayla discovered that the problem seems to occur in the functioning of the brain. She learned that, as humans, we need different parts of our brain to work together all the time so that we may understand our surroundings and be able to react to what is happening. For example, if you see or hear something funny you will laugh. Your brain has helped you to understand what was funny and to respond by laughing. Your brain does not tell you to laugh when someone has gotten into a serious accident, however. Instead, you are driven to be afraid, sad and run to help perhaps. Autistic children seem to have areas in their brain that may not be connected properly. They are not able to attach what is happening to a specific emotion, or to connect symbols such as letters to its name and sound.

From these observations and research findings, something quite amazing happened. Kayla decided to test her idea for helping Lorena by gently inviting her younger cousin to sit with her at the piano during one of their family gatherings. At first, Lorena was afraid of the piano keys, but she overcame this fear when Kayla placed her cousin's hand on top of her own and allowed Lorena to press gently on her fingers to play the notes. Soon, Lorena learned that there was nothing to be afraid of and she began to play the keys on her own - using her own fingers to touch the keys.

Kayla began by showing Lorena that a certain key or note of the piano represented a particular letter of the English alphabet. Since her cousin only knew six letters of the alphabet when they began, Kayla first had to teach her cousin to recognize a letter by seeing it and then playing the key on the piano for that letter. For example, Lorena was asked to play the letter "L" as Kayla pointed to the letter placed atop a piano key, while her cousin would carefully look at the letter card and play the key for the letter "L". Eventually, Lorena learned to connect all 26 letters of the alphabet with the piano key and sound for that letter. Amazingly, she came to know when she had made a mistake simply by the sound of the note on the piano – even when those notes were beside one another and may not have sounded that different!

Kayla then decided that Lorena was ready to take the next important step. She taught her cousin that each letter and its sound on the piano could be put together to make "words". If Kayla wanted Lorena to "play" the notes or keys that made up the word "Lion", she would first say the word and show Lorena the picture of the animal with the word "Lion" spelled above the picture. Kayla's cousin began to recognize the words and was able to "spell" the word on the piano by hearing the word, seeing its spelling, and then matching the keys on the piano that corresponded to the letters that made up the word "Lion". By learning to play the notes on the piano that spelled the word "Lion" Lorena was mastering reading and spelling! "I thought that if she could learn to read and spell it would create a shared bond with her cousins, help her to better communicate her thoughts and wishes and help her to participate more fully in the world around her," Kayla explains on her website.

Once Kayla taught her younger cousin the important skill of reading and spelling a selection of nouns and verbs that were placed together (such as "Lion – Roars") using the piano, she created another important step in her teaching program. Because autistic children often have difficulty understanding emotions, Kayla created a way for Lorena to "read" the emotions of some of the animals whose name and spelling she had already mastered. Her cousin would have to learn to recognize and identify certain emotions such as happy, sad, angry, afraid, surprised and disgusting.

The Story of Little Bear is a forty-page book that Kayla wrote to introduce autistic children to the emotions that we all experience. Within the story are illustrations and words that take the child along on the adventure of Little Bear as he experiences these different emotions. The autistic child notices the changing expressions on Bear's face and plays the musical sounds that go along with that emotion. For example, in one part of the story, Little Bear becomes "angry" that the other bears have taken his honey. There are three part **harmonies** that represent each of the six emotions. The child would play the three part harmony for the "angry" face in this case. The child hears the musical sounds or harmony for that emotion.

The Story of Little Bear is a remarkable book that has helped Lorena and other children experiencing autism to recognize, identify and understand the normal emotions of all people. This will help them come to a better understanding of their own emotions and that of others – like which emotions go along with certain situations in our life.

The further along Kayla went with her development of her teaching system, the more she came to realize she was on to something quite amazing. She named her idea *Sounds Into Syllables®* and underwent preparations to enter her concept into a science fair for high school students in Ontario, the most populated province in Canada. Her grade 7 and 8 teacher, Mrs.Perino, served as Kayla's mentor, helping her to understand how she needed to prepare if she was to present her idea successfully at the fair.

*Kayla presents
Sounds Into Syllables*

Mrs. Perino had not, in all her years of teaching, encountered such a dedicated, determined, hard-working and talented student as Kayla. She remembers Kayla as a true leader who completed all her other assignments to the highest level of excellence using all her talents - even her artistic ones - to help her. In fact, Kayla's other school assignments were completed with such wonderful detail and presentation that many of them were entered into other contests as well!

Kayla's success with *Sounds Into Syllables®* began to be noticed by those in the scientific and medical fields, especially the field of autism. She was invited to present her idea at various conferences and competitions across Canada. She won many of these competitions and spoke confidently and passionately at all the events. Newspaper articles with her story gradually emerged across Ontario and all of Canada.

Soon she was noticed by one of the largest media news companies in the world, CNN. Her story was featured in a CNN news segment called "Impact Your World". People from around the world were able to hear about the amazing accomplishment of a young teenager from Canada who had developed a teaching system to help autistic children read, spell, and communicate, thereby helping them to build more confidence in themselves. Many of these people voted for Kayla to win a CNN *Heroes* award for her outstanding contribution in the field of autism. She won! Kayla was extremely proud when she received her award on stage in front of many individuals from all over our planet who were working hard to help the most disadvantaged peoples of our world. It was truly an amazing experience!

Eventually, Kayla's dream of introducing her teaching system to more autistic children across Canada and the United States would come true. After witnessing the success of the system with her cousin Lorena, and receiving the approval of many experts in the field of autism, Kayla was confident that her idea would help many others who are limited by similar autistic difficulties. This way, she could also research how well her teaching system was performing with other autistic children while making it more available to those who could benefit from it. Kayla believes that "opening the pathways to communication is the key to helping children with autism function in the world around them."

Today, *Sounds Into Syllables*® has been used successfully in various classrooms in North America. Kayla's research has shown that other children, like her cousin Lorena, are also improving in their reading, spelling and communication skills. She has received encouraging **feedback** from teachers and parents of autistic children. Results seem to show that these children are also improving in their attention span and therefore are able to focus on, and complete tasks for longer periods of time - something that many autistic children struggle with.

Kayla's contribution to the world of autism research and understanding is very important. She has shown us that we can bridge arts - such as music - with helping in the advancement of medical discoveries – such as helping autistic children with abnormal brain functions to spell, read and communicate. How amazing that she accomplished all this while still a teenager!

"Seeing these kids overcome barriers is huge," Kayla had said in a *TeenFlare* magazine article. It has been, and continues to be, a rewarding and encouraging experience for Kayla who has worked hard to develop her teaching system. The success she has experienced and the awards she has won are all the result of her dedication to improving the lives of her autistic cousin and many others with similar challenges. Her grade 7 and 8 teacher, Mrs. Perino, declares that, "The people who Kayla is helping will be able to communicate their thanks to her one day – something that they may never have had a chance to do before."

Kayla saw an opportunity to help and she took action to make a difference in a way that is very important. She believes that all children have the opportunity to find something that they care deeply about and to get involved to make a difference as well. Her advice to kids is that, "If you have an idea, go with it! No matter what it is - lean on family,  friends, and teachers to help in any way."

Kayla (right) with Lorena (left)

Today, Kayla is attending Stanford University in California where she continues to be recognized for her important contribution in the field of autism research and understanding. Her teaching system, *Sounds Into Syllables*®, has won 50 awards worldwide! As well, she would like all children to know that autistic kids are wonderful people and that once you get to know them you will enjoy their unique personality and energy. Often, autistic children need opportunities to practice their social interaction with other children who are not autistic. For this reason, many autistic children are placed into regular schools and spend time in regular classrooms. Perhaps then, the amazing opportunity to meet and get to know an autistic child may present itself to you one day.

What You Should Know:

Autism is part of a group of disorders known as autism spectrum disorders (ASD). Today, 1 in 110 individuals is diagnosed with autism, making it more common than pediatric cancer, diabetes, and AIDS combined. It occurs in all racial, ethnic, and social groups and is four times more likely to strike boys than girls. Symptoms can range from very mild to quite severe.

The true cause of autism is unknown. However, scientific evidence shows a link between **genetic** components and environmental factors.

Because Autism is the fastest growing **developmental disability** in North America, more research and education is needed to fully understand the various causes and treatment of the disorder.

Autistic children are often very bright individuals who often display gifts or talents in one or more areas, even as they may be delayed in others. With patience and support, individuals can help an autistic child realize and use these special abilities.

Autistic children need a lot of **structure** and routine in their lives so that they understand what is expected and acceptable in social situations.

How You Can Help:

Consider doing your own research on childhood autism. You may use your findings to educate your family, friends, and classmates. You may also consider presenting your findings during a class science project, where you explore the link between our brain and our behaviour. Perhaps you may explore your own idea for helping autistic children in some way.

"Toonies for Autism" and "Cycle for Autism" are two great ways to get involved in helping to raise awareness and funds to help in research and treatment of autistic kids. For more information visit, www.autismsociety.on.ca where you will learn how your family, school and community can help to make a difference in the lives of autistic children and their families.

Read _Sometimes My Brother: Helping Kids Understand Autism through a Sibling's Eyes_ by Angie Healy (Publisher: Future Horizons). Spend time discussing the book with your family and classmates. You may examine the advantages and disadvantages of having a sibling or a cousin with autism. You can draw a VENN diagram and list all the different characteristics and abilities of yourself versus that of an autistic child. In the center of the diagram, find ways that you are similar to an autistic child.

Check out these websites to learn more about childhood autism:

www.autismspeaks.org

www.kidshealth.org/kid/health_problems/brain/autism.html

www.autism.about.com

You may visit Kayla's website www.soundsintosyllables.com to learn more about her teaching system for autistic kids.

Sounds Into Syllables ® is a registered trademark; patent is pending.

Craig Battles Child Labour

Chapter 5

"Children aren't simply empty vessels waiting to be filled; we're people with ideas, talents, opinions, and dreams." Craig Kielburger

Many of you may have heard of Craig Kielburger, especially if you have been a witness to the amazing **WE DAY** events that celebrate the power of young people to create positive change in the world, and which take place across Canada every year. But do you actually know how Craig's story began? His story unfolded in an unusual and unexpected way – that's what makes it quite amazing! Here is how it all began . . . .

It was a typical weekday morning when twelve-year old Craig Kielburger sat down at his breakfast table and began devouring his favourite cereal. As he ate, he launched into a search through The Toronto Star newspaper for the comics he loved best. However, he never quite made it to the comics section that day. Instead, something very real and very different found him, and in that moment, Craig's life would take an unexpected turn and change forever.

On that morning, in that newspaper, a photograph of a young boy wearing a red vest with his hands reaching up in the air while flashing what seemed to be a triumphant smile, caught Craig's eye. However, it was the caption found with that picture that drew Craig's attention further and would begin one of the most amazing journeys of compassion ever undertaken by a Canadian child.

The title of the newspaper article read, "Battled Child Labour, Boy, 12, Murdered." As Craig began to read who this young boy was and what had happened to him, he felt a deep sense of sadness for this person he had never met.

The young boy in the photo was 12 year old Iqbal Masih of Pakistan. Craig learned that, at the age of four, Iqbal had been sold into slavery by his parents who were quite poor and needed money. This little boy had to work many long hours, from morning until night, weaving carpets that would be sold mainly to tourists and other countries around the world. Tying tiny knots that would make the carpets was quite exhausting work. Iqbal was not given the opportunity to play or to go to school. He was not given enough food to eat which may explain why he appeared so small for his age. Although he was very tired and his fingers hurt, he was not able to rest. This brave little boy tried to run away, but he was caught and brought back to continue working in the factory. He was even shackled with chains so that he could not run away again.

Iqbal worked as a child labourer for six long years until a man named Ehsan Ulla Khan who worked for a human rights organization in Pakistan helped him to escape. Iqbal was then ten years old and began attending the school operated by Mr. Khan's organization.

The picture that Craig was looking at in the newspaper that morning was taken when Iqbal was speaking up against the horrors of child labour in his country. Iqbal traveled all over the world telling people about his life in the carpet factory in the hope that everyone would know what was happening and perhaps be moved to help other children in similar situations. Sadly however, Iqbal would not live to see the impact his life had had on many others. When he returned to his country after one of his trips, he was murdered. Someone did not like that he was speaking up against the carpet industry and its child workers.

Craig immediately noticed the huge difference in his life to the harsh life Iqbal had led. They were both boys and both twelve years old, but that was where the similarities seemed to end. Craig had friends whom he could hang out with, he went to school and he ran on the cross-country team. In his short life, Iqbal had endured a lot of suffering as a child slave worker but had tried to make a difference before he died. His amazing story captured Craig's heart and inspired Craig to do something to make a difference as well!

Craig asked his teacher if he could make a presentation to his class. Although he was nervous speaking in front of his fellow classmates, Craig mustered up the courage and explained to everyone what he had learned in the Iqbal Masih newspaper article. This simple act began his quest to bring attention and awareness to the issue of child labour around the world, and in so doing, he would carry on the work of brave Iqbal Masih.

After his presentation, Craig asked if any of the students would like to help him with this very serious and important problem. When some of his classmates raised their hands, Free The Children, an organization to help bring an end to child labour around the world was founded. Craig and his friends then began by signing petitions and faxing world leaders, including their own Prime Minister of Canada. They raised money for their organization through garage sales, bake sales, soda pop sales and car washes.

People began to hear of Craig and his friends and what they were doing. Most people were very impressed with them, however, some adults felt that they were too young to be speaking about child labour and that they did not fully understand the problem. Everyone at Free The Children worked hard to let people know that you are never too young to help those who need it, especially children. "Every young person has an issue that hits them in the heart," says Craig. "But I believe that society has taught them they don't have the power to change things; that they have to wait until they're adults to achieve results."

One of the first goals that Craig and his friends set for themselves was to convince the Canadian government to label the rugs or carpets that were not made by children and encourage people to buy these ones only. That way, the people who use children to make the carpets would loose money and perhaps be forced out of business.

As the activities of Craig and his friends grew, his home became the world headquarters for Free The Children. Thousands of children from around the world began to hear of what they were doing and wanted to get involved to help bring an end to child labour practices worldwide. Children from countries such as Canada, the United States, Pakistan, India, Mexico, Brazil and Ghana wrote letters to Free The Children asking what they can do to help, or telling what they were already doing to help.

A burning desire to meet some of the children he was fighting for drove Craig to the next important step in his young life. He wanted to go to South Asia, however, his parents were not happy with the idea. They told him he was too young and the trip was too dangerous for a twelve-year old. Fortunately, a twenty-four year old man named Alam Rahman who was studying at the University of Toronto decided to take a year off from school to travel to South Asia to find out more about his roots. He invited

Craig to accompany him on his trip which would take them to Bangladesh, India, Thailand and Pakistan. Alam could speak the languages and act as a chaperone for Craig. Craig's parents liked Alam and trusted him very much. They allowed their son to go to South Asia with him.

After careful planning and preparation, Craig and Alam set off on an incredible trip that would bring the world to the doors of Free The Children, opening it to show the misery of child labour in many countries. During the two months that they traveled around South Asia meeting and speaking with factory owners and the child workers, Craig learned more than he ever could by only reading articles or looking at documentaries of child labourers on TV.

He found children working in many different areas - not only

 in factories. Some worked in homes, helping to cook and clean. Others worked on the fishing docks, loading and unloading cargo. Many children could be found in farm fields and garbage landfills. Most of these children worked all day without a break to rest. Some were able to take a break to attend a nearby school for a short time and then return to work.

What Craig realized was that the conditions that many of these children worked under were absolutely horrible. Many of these children were injured or even killed on the job because they worked with dangerous instruments or machines. Many were treated badly by the factory owners or supervisors who watched them carefully to make sure they kept working. Craig wrote down everything he was learning in a journal to share with everyone back home and around the world.

When he returned two months later to Toronto, he was greeted at the airport by cheering people, TV camera lights, and signs waving that said, "Welcome Home Craig" and, "We're Behind You All the Way". TV news stations, talk shows, newspapers and magazines all demanded interviews with him. His trip had brought much needed attention to the issue of child labourers and Craig was determined to use the spotlight to let the world know that we must work together to end this terrible problem.

Craig speaks to children during his trip to South Asia

Free The Children exploded into an international movement of young people taking action to help other young people who could not help themselves. At times, they were not given the opportunity to speak their voice in front of important adult leaders. Despite this, Craig and his friends continued their fight on behalf of these exploited children, using whatever **platform** they could stand on to get their voices heard. Craig wrote a book called Free the Children about his experiences since reading about Iqbal Masih in the newspaper that morning. Adult leaders were encouraged to accept that young people could play an important role in changing the world for better.

Soon after Craig's return to Canada, one of Free The Children's next projects was to help fund a rehabilitation center that takes in Pakistani children who have escaped child labour. Some of the money for this rehabilitation center was the result of a school fundraiser, where students donated as many coins as they could manage. The center provides shelter and a school for the children. Through education, these children will be able to understand their rights and work hard to overcome their poverty.

Some countries started to adopt the Rugmark label, a tag that is placed on carpets to declare that child labour was not involved in its manufacture. Free The Children encouraged Canadians to be aware that some of the things we buy, such as brand name clothing, carpets and sports equipment, were made by child slave workers in developing countries.

Craig's efforts and his determination to continue the work of Free The Children caught the attention of important individuals around the world who also care about the children who live in these sad conditions. He made appearances on talk shows like the Oprah Winfrey Show; he met the Dalai Lama of Tibet, former US Vice President Al Gore and former US President Bill Clinton, Queen Noor of Jordan and leaders of many other countries including his own Prime Minister of Canada.

Craig's message to all these important adults was that, "Children aren't simply empty vessels waiting to be filled; we're people with ideas, talents, opinions, and dreams", and the dream was for the elimination of child labour throughout the world. All children deserve the same opportunities to play, learn, laugh and grow into the adults they aspire to be. This is an important message of Free The Children. It was the message of Iqbal Masih's life.

Today, Craig is a young man in his twenties, working hard to empower young people to make a difference in improving conditions in their communities and around the world. He and Free The Children have won many awards, including being nominated for the Nobel Peace Prize four times! The organization has built over 650 schools helping to keep children in classrooms and out of child labour. But there is still much work to be done. Craig continues to travel the globe speaking to people about

Craig protesting child labour during his trip to South Asia

his dream of a world where all children can be free and have the opportunity to go to school, no matter where they live. One of his recent books, which he wrote with his older brother Mark, is titled Me to We. The book has created a social movement that inspires all people to find their own gift in contributing to make a better world.

What You Should Know:

About 220 million children between the ages of 5 and 17 are engaged in child labor around the world.

Over 132 million girls and boys under 15 years old work on farms and plantations, handling machinery, sowing and harvesting crops, spraying pesticides and tending livestock. They work under dangerous and unhealthy situations.

Photo by africa (FreeDigitalPhotos.net)

About 14 percent (almost 32 million) of children in India ages 5-14 are involved in child labor activities, including carpet production.

There are 5.7 million child labourers in Latin America and the Caribbean.

600 million children live in extreme poverty around the world.

The problems of extreme poverty, high population, food shortage, illness and conflict within a country are the main reasons that child labour exists in continents such as Africa.

How You Can Help:

Learn more about what the issues surrounding child labour in developing countries are. Why does child labour exist? Investigate reasons for the circumstances surrounding children working to help provide for their families. How can these children help their families and still be given the important opportunity of education? How does access to education break the cycle of poverty?

You, your school and/or your family can organize a fundraiser, such as a bake sale or a community garage sale. The dollars you raise can help support international development projects around the world through Free The Children (see www.freethechildren. com for many details).

Ask your principal if your school can join the movement towards global awareness and action and join the *We Schools in Action Program* (see www.freethechildren.com/weschools/).

Photo by africa
(FreeDigitalPhotos.net)

Your school can *Adopt a Village* with Free The Children! Your school will receive lots of fun and interactive fundraising materials to help you raise money for a specific international development project in Kenya, China, Sri Lanka, Sierra Leone, and other areas around the world.

Your family can choose to use your travel experiences as a way to give back. Visit an orphanage, help build a school and get involved in making a difference in the lives of others. Visit www. freethechildren.com/getinvolved/family/ for ideas.

You can volunteer overseas with your school group through Free The Children. Learn more here: www.freethechildren.com/getinvolved/volunteeroverseas/.

Sign up and take the *Vow of Silence* on November 30th of every year, and stand in solidarity with children who are silenced by poverty, disease and exploitation. Your vow will raise awareness and funds for these special children.

You can also check out Craig and Mark's website *www.metowe.com* for more ideas on how to get involved and take action in your community and around the world.

Learn more about Craig and the work of Free The Children on YouTube, Facebook and Twitter:

http://www.youtube.com/freethechildrenintl

http://www.facebook.com/freethechildren

http://www.facebook.com/craigkielburger

http://www.facebook.com/weday

http://twitter.com/freethechildren

http://twitter.com/craigkielburger

Other Facts and Statistics on Childhood Illnesses and Natural Disasters, and How You Can Help:

About HIV and AIDS:

In 2009, globally, there were 2 million children below the age of 15 living with HIV.

Globally, AIDS-related illnesses remain one of the leading causes of death and are expected to continue as a significant global cause of childhood mortality in the coming decades.

Every day, about 2,500 young people acquire HIV. In 2009 alone, an estimated 890, 000 young people were newly infected with the virus.

In most countries, children who have lost both parents to HIV and AIDS are less likely to be in school than children whose parents are both still alive.

Photo by africa
(FreeDigitalPhotos.net)

About Vaccinations:

Despite significant progress in reducing childhood mortality, nearly two million children still die each year from vaccine-preventable diseases.

UNICEF is the leading global provider of disease-preventing bed nets and vaccines. UNICEF-supplied vaccines reach over half the world's children and save millions of lives.

UNICEF Executive Director, Anthony Lake, says that "We have the vaccines and the expertise to save millions of children's lives. Now we must match our knowledge with our commitment to help the poorest, most vulnerable children."

About Natural Disasters:

*US Navy by Photographer's Mate 2nd
Class Elizabeth A. Edwards*

In the countries of Asia and the Pacific, such as Myanmar, China and Pakistan, natural disasters are expected to become even more frequent because of population growth, **urbanization**, deforestation and **climate change**.

"Unless we act now, we will see more disasters due to unplanned urbanization and environmental degradation. And weather-related disasters are sure to rise in the future, due to factors that include climate change," says Margareta Wahlström, UN General for Disaster Risk Reduction.

Developing nations often do not have the resources they need or the ability to cope with natural disasters and their aftermath.

Children are more likely to die during natural disasters or, later, due to malnutrition, injuries or deadly diseases. For those that survive, their development is jeopardized. Children can also suffer greatly from the emotional and **economic consequences** of natural disasters.

Climate change is expected to increase the harshness and frequency of weather-related natural hazards such as storms, high rainfalls, floods, droughts and heat-waves. Together with sea level rise, this will lead to more disasters in the future – unless prompt action is taken.

How You Can Help:

When a natural disaster strikes any part of our world, waste no time in organizing, planning, raising awareness and fundraising to help relief efforts. Discuss how climate changes effects the occurrence of natural disasters.

Brainstorm ideas with your family members, classmates and teachers for ways that your family or school can get involved in the causes of children worldwide. Pick a cause - such as childhood illness in developing countries - research as much as possible to learn more, become passionate and set goals that you can achieve.

You can donate proceeds from school events such as annual BBQs, bake sales, Readathons, and Spelling Bees to a worthwhile cause. You can also raise funds by charging $1 to watch students versus teachers in a sporting event of your choice.

Instead of presents, your family members, teachers and friends may love to receive a "Gift in Kind", where you donate a certain amount of money on their behalf to a charity.

Find a cause you are passionate about and volunteer your time to help out.

Check out the **UNICEF** website for information on programs, fundraising ideas and many more interesting facts for children and youth, www.unicef.ca

U.S. Navy by Photographer's Mate
2nd Class Elizabeth A. Edwards

Glossary of Terms

abuse – to use something improperly or wrongly

affordable housing – usually housing in which a household is able to pay for (while taking into consideration the size, safety and cleanliness of the property)

ambassador – a citizen who has been selected to hold a position of high rank to represent the causes of a country or a major international organization such as the United Nations

autism – a problem occurring in the brain that makes it difficult for some children to communicate and function normally

biodiverse – the many different types of plant and animal life found in a particular habitat or ecosystem throughout the world

biofuels – fuel that is made from plants grown today and are therefore a renewable resource

biome – a large area on the earth that is defined by the plants and animals that live there - a rainforest is a biome

blog – an online journal or diary that is shared through a website

capacity – capable of performing or producing to have adequate growth

carpet industry – a type of business activity having to do with the manufacturing and finishing of carpets and rugs which will then be sold to individuals or businesses around the world

child mortality – refers to the number of deaths of children between the ages of 1 to 12 or in a certain population or geographical area – majority of deaths occur between the ages of 1 to 5

child soldier – the participation of children in armed conflict or struggles and who may serve as spies or slaves for the group that has control over them

climate change - any change in global temperatures and precipitation over time due to natural or human causes – can also be known as global warming

conflict – a struggle or battle within a country between opposing groups of people who are organized and use military weapons to overthrow each other

cryobiology – the study of the effects of extremely low temperatures on living organisms and cells - in many cases, to understand how to "freeze", store and preserve them

cyclone – a violent wind storm that rotates either counterclockwise or clockwise and usually comes along with destructive weather

developing countries – countries that are poor and whose citizens are mostly agricultural workers, but that wants to become more advanced socially and economically

developmental – having to do with normal changes that children undergo as they move through infancy, childhood and adolescents (such as learning to walk and talk as toddlers)

developmental disability – usually having to do with a lack of a given mental or physical ability that is observed before the age of 18

economic consequences – the way a state or nation distributes its resources (such as goods and services) to its citizens at times of war, a disaster or other unforeseen event

electronic waste (e-waste) – discarded electrical or electronic devices

exploited children – children who are used or victimized in some way for someone else's gain

extinction – a particular plant or animal species has died out and is no longer alive anywhere in the world – natural or human activities can be the cause

feedback – like an evaluation, it is information that is given back to someone to let them know the results of a test, an activity, or a program

financial – having to do with matters of money

fossil fuels – the decomposed remains of plant and animals formed over millions of years beneath the earth and used as a source of energy – coal, oil and natural gas are fossil fuels

Free Geek – a nonprofit community organization that reduces the environmental impact of waste electronics by reusing and recycling donated technology while at the same time, helping to reduce the movement of hazardous waste throughout the world.

genetic – tending to occur among family members or a species usually by heredity (dealing with passing traits or characteristics from parent to child)

global deforestation – the cutting down and clearing away of large areas of forest in parts of the world

greenhouse gas – gases, such as carbon dioxide, in the earth's atmosphere traps the energy (heat) of the sun and excessive amounts of these gases prevent some of this heat to escape back into space thereby causing the earth to become warmer

harmonies – a combination of musical notes or sounds that is considered pleasing to the ears

homeless mission – a charitable organization that provides shelter, meals, clothing and other means of assistance for those living in poverty and without a home

HIV-AIDS – Human Immunodeficiency Virus (HIV) and Acquired Immune Deficiency Syndrome (AIDS which is the name given to the disease associated with HIV) - a virus invades the immune system of humans causing severe illness that can lead to death

humanitarian – having to do with assisting and providing for the welfare of human beings who are in great need

human rights – the rights and freedoms to which all human beings are entitled

iMovie – a filmmaker or video editing software developed by Apple Inc. for their Mac computers and iPad

income – the sum of all the monetary earnings (or money) someone receives in a certain time period

international development projects – projects that involve the development of greater quality of life for humans in need around the world

latrines – toilettes used by communities in the developing world to allow for safe and hygienic means of human urination and defecation

livelihood – means of supporting oneself and/or a family usually by working to earn income or by trading items

low income – monetary earnings are not enough to support an individual or family – usually associated with **poverty** which is the lack of basic human needs, such as clean water, nutrition, health care, education, clothing and shelter, because of the inability to afford them

manufacture - the use of machines, tools and human labour to produce goods for use or sale

microorganisms – tiny, one-celled organisms such as viruses, fungi and bacteria that are found in all living things – some can be harmful, while others are necessary for the survival of living things

Millennium Development Goals – 8 goals that the United Nations and its members have agreed to achieve by the year 2015 - they include reducing extreme poverty, reducing child mortality rates, and fighting disease epidemics such as AIDS.

Nobel Peace Prize – named after Swedish industrialist and inventor Alfred Nobel – it is an international prize given to individuals who do great work in bringing nations together and promoting peace

photosynthesis – the process by which plants capture and use light energy, to convert carbon dioxide, water, and minerals from soil to make food and thereby releases oxygen back into the air

platform – using an opportunity to express your ideas or opinions about something

resources – something physical (such as a food bank) or a service (such as counseling homeless individuals) that only has limited availability and that benefits those who use them

rural – refers to farming or country communities, areas beyond the city and its suburbs

sanitation – acts to promote proper hygiene and cleanliness when it comes to human wastes in order to prevent illness and disease

social action – refers to the actions or reactions of individuals and/or people in a society – individuals working to raise awareness on an issue effecting their community are taking social action

social interaction – having to do with relationships that involve communication between individuals which can be verbal or non-verbal (two children playing together are engaged in social interaction)

social movement – a type of group action focused on a political or social issue and that hopes to bring about positive change

social responsibility – the idea that an organization, group of people, or individual should act to help society and/or the world as a whole

structure – in a social setting it has to do with predictable and unchanged patterns and relationships (such as the schedule that one follows at school on a daily or weekly basis)

sustain – to provide for and support a person/group by supplying necessities and nourishments in order to prevent illness or death over a long-term period

toxic – a substance that is capable of causing injury or death, especially by chemical means; poisonous

tsunami – giant ocean waves that are brought on by an undersea earthquake or volcanic eruption

UNICEF – refers to the United Nations Children's Fund which is a United Nations (UN) organization. UNICEF is the world's leading child focused humanitarian and development agency working to ensure every child has every chance, with no exceptions.

urbanization – a rapid and massive growth of urban areas (cities) caused by people moving from rural areas (country side) into the larger cities typically looking for a better life

Acknowledgements/Credits

(# refers to order of the fact's appearance in What You Should Know)

Ryan Hreljac: Ryan and the Water Well

Book Reference: *Ryan and Jimmy And the Well in Africa That Brought Them Together* by Herb Shoveller (see website for more information: http://www.ryanswell.ca/get-involved/merchandise.aspx)

<u>What You Should Know:</u>

#1) World Health Organization/UNICEF Progress on Sanitation and Drinking Water, 2010 Update: http://www.wssinfo.org/fileadmin/user_upload/resources/1278061137-JMP_report_2010_en.pdf

#2) World Health Organization: http://www.who.int/water_sanitation_health/hygiene/en/

#3) World Health Organization: http://whqlibdoc.who.int/publications/2010/9789241599351_eng_Part1a.pdf

#4) World Health Organization: http://www.who.int/water_
sanitation_health/hygiene/en/

#5) UN Millennium Development Project: http://www.
unmillenniumproject.org/documents/MainReportChapter15-
lowres.pdf

#6) World Health Organization:http://whqlibdoc.who.int/
publications/2010/9789241599351_eng_Part1a.pdf

#7) http://www.unwater.org/downloads/UN-Water_GLAAS_
2010_Report.pdf ndp.org/en/reports/global/hdr2006/

Photo Image Credits:

Photos of Ryan courtesy of the Ryan's Well Foundation
(www.ryanswell.ca)

Chapter Cover Page Quote from: http://www.ryanswell.ca/
media/rwf-blog/kids-are-amazing!.aspx

Miranda Andersen: Miranda Films for the Environment

Quoted directly from:

#1) Source: http://www.unep.org/pdf/UNEP_Profile/Ecosystem_
management.pdf

#2,3) Source: http://www.pcrf.org/reeffacts.html

#4-6) Source: http://www.unep.org/pdf/BlueCarbon_screen_
english.pdf

#7) Source: http://environment.nationalgeographic.com/environment/global-warming/deforestation-overview/

#8) Source: http://environment.nationalgeographic.com/environment/global-warming/deforestation-overview/

#9) Source: http://www.greenpeace.org/international/en/campaigns/toxics/electronics/

Quotes about Dr. Mary Hagedorn's work taken from *Meet Our Scientist: Mary Hagedorn – Coral Science* uploaded on *YouTube* by *Smithsonian Science*; and http://smithsonianscience.org/2011/05/smithsonian-conservation-biology-institute-to-create-frozen-repository-for-the-great-barrier-reef/.

Photo Image Credits:

All photos courtesy of Miranda Andersen.

Hannah Taylor: Hannah Cares for the Homeless

Internet References: http://speeches.empireclub.org/62873/data?n=1; http://money.howstuffworks.com/do-something-brick-awards-winner-hannah-taylor.htm; www.ladybugfoundation.ca

What You Should Know: About Homelessness in Canada

Source: Calgary-based Sheldon Chumir Foundation for Ethics in Leadership, journalist and author Gordon Laird comments on new report, June 26, 2007
Source: http://intraspec.ca/homelessCanada.php

What You Should Know: About Homelessness Around the World

#1) Source: http://www.unhabitat.org (Habitat Agenda)

#2) Source: Universal Declaration of Human Rights: http://www.un.org/en/documents/udhr/index.shtml

Photo Image Credits:

Photos of Hannah courtesy of www.ladybugfoundation.ca

Kayla Cornale: Kayla Opens a Window for World of Autism

What You Should Know:

#1-2) Source: http://www.autismspeaks.org/what-autism

Photo Image Credits:

Photos of Kayla courtesy of Kayla Cornale

Chapter Cover Page Quote from: 2009 phone interview with Sheneeza Kanji

Craig Kielburger: Craig Battles Child Labour

Books References: *Free the Children* by Craig Kielburger; *Me to We* by Craig and Mark

Kielburger (For more information on both books and other Me to We books see website: http://www.freethechildren.com/getinvolved/books/)

Also see:

Craig Kielburger, Remarkable Canadians Series, by Bryan Pezzi, Weigl Educational Publishers Limited (2007), Calgary, Alberta, Canada

Sources for Iqbal Masih:

http://history1900s.about.com/od/1990s/a/IqbalMasih.htm; http://www.mirrorimage.com/iqbal/

References for Iqbal Masih:

Kuklin, Susan. Iqbal Masih and the Crusaders Against Child Slavery. Henry Holt and Company, New York, 1998. Deitz Shea, Pegi. The Carpet Boy's Gift. Tilbury House Publishers, Maine, 2003.

<u>What You Should Know:</u>

#1-2) Source: International Labour Organization, "The end of child labour: Within reach", 2006 with added reference to: http://www.ilo.org/public/english/support/lib/resource/subject/childlabor.htm

#3-5) Source: *The State of the World's Children 2006*, UNICEF

Other Facts and Statistics on Childhood Illnesses and Natural Disasters, and How You Can Help:

What You Should Know About HIV:

#1) UNICEF International: http://www.unicef.org/aids/index_preventionMTCT.html

#2) UNICEF, Child Info: http://www.childinfo.org/hiv_aids.html

#3-4) Opportunity in Crisis: Preventing HIV from early adolescence to early adulthood: http://www.unicef.org/aids/index_58689.html

What You Should Know About Vaccinations:

#1) UNICEF International
http://www.unicef.org/media/media_58919.html

#2) Progress for Children No. 9
http://www.unicef.org/media/files/Progress_for_Children-No.9_EN_081710.pdf

#3-4) Source: UNICEF International (http://unicef.org/media/media 58919.html)

What You Should Know About Natural Disasters:

#1) http://www.unicef.org/eapro/activities_3618.html

#2) http://www.unisdr.org/we/advocate/climate-change

Cover globe image: Salvatore Vuono/FreeDigitalPhotos.net; African children images: Africa/FreeDigitalPhotos.net; Buddhist child smiling image: Worradmu/FreeDigitalPhotos.net; Girl writing exam image: Koratmember/FreeDigitalPhotosnet.

Additional internet/book references available on author website at authorhouse.com

The author gratefully acknowledges the help of UNICEF Canada with many of the UN facts and statistics.

The author wishes to thank the parents, organizations and the "Amazing Canadian Kids" represented in this book. Without their support and amazing stories, this book would not have been possible. Thank you for doing what you do to make the world a better place.

Many thanks especially to Angelique Richardson, Benita Hansraj, Ruth Foster, Jennifer Whiffin, Dr. Mary Hagedorn and Beth Campbell.